RACCOON

Sandie Lee Books

The Raccoon

The raccoon, or sometimes called, a coon, is the largest species in the procyonid family. Some native peoples call this animal, ahrah-koon-em. This means, "one who rubs, scrubs and scratches with its hands." The first known species of the raccoon lived about 25 million years-ago in Europe. There are 4 sub-species of the raccoon. However, they all look very similar to each other. Let's dig into more fun facts about the raccoon to explore its world.

Where in the World?

Did you know the raccoon is a very common animal? This animal can be found throughout North America. It prefers areas with lots of trees and near a water source. This can include mountainous regions, marshlands and even urban areas. In fact, the raccoon can be considered a pest in some neighborhoods.

The Body of a Raccoon

Did you know the raccoon can measure up to 28 inches long? An adult male raccoon can weigh up to 20 pounds. This animal is probably most recognized by its black facial "mask." It has a medium-length tail with black rings around it. It has shorter legs and 4 paws with claws on each one.

The Raccoon's Fur

Did you know the raccoon's fur is very thick? The coat on the raccoon has a dense undercoat and longer top hairs. It is mostly greyish in color with some black intermixed. Its coat keeps it well insulated and warm in the cold winter months. Raccoons also have a slight musky scent.

The Raccoon's Hands

Did you know the raccoon uses its front paws like hands? The front paws of the raccoon have 4 long fingers and a thumb-like digit. This animal can pick up objects with its hands. The raccoon has a very strong sense of touch and will use its paws to identify things.

What the Raccoon Eats

Did you know the raccoon is an omnivore? This means the raccoon will eat both meat and plant matter. In fact, the raccoon will eat most anything from insects, fruit, nuts, acorns, bird eggs and even people's garbage. This species is very good at opening lids of garbage cans and raiding bird feeders.

The Raccoon's Special

Did you know the raccoon douses? This is when the raccoon will pick up its food and appear to be washing it. When near a water source, the raccoon fishes food out of the water and will turn it over in its hands. Since its paws are so sensitive, this is partly how the raccoon tests its food.

Raccoons at Rest

Did you know this animal is mostly active at night? This is called being, nocturnal. The raccoon will spend the daytime hours resting in trees or in rocky locations. Sometimes, a raccoon in an urban area may take up residence in or under people's sheds or decks. The raccoon has also been found in attics and in barns.

Racoons at Play

Did you know raccoons engage in playful behaviour? The baby raccoons will venture out of the den and play with each other. They will run, chase, tumble and nip at one another. It is through play that baby raccoons learn to forage for food and to use their little hands.

The Raccoon as Prey

Did you know the raccoon is hunted by many species? Even though the raccoon will ferociously protect itself by biting and scratching, it does have natural enemies. Large land animals like the bobcat, coyotes, wolves and cougars will all hunt the coon. Man has also hunted this animal for its pelt.

The Raccoon as Predator

Did you know the raccoon will raid bird nests? This species of animal loves the taste of bird and snake eggs. Once it locates a nest of eggs, it will steal them away. The raccoon will also hunt smaller domesticated animals, like kittens and baby chickens. It is best to keep your small pets away from raccoons.

Raccoon Talk

Did you know the raccoon has a variety of calls? This animal can hiss, snort and make a barking sound when it feels afraid. An angry raccoon can growl, snarl and squeal. A baby raccoon will make a squeaking sound when it is being nipped or disciplined by the mother raccoon.

Mom Raccoon

Did you know the female raccoon can have babies when she is only 1 year-old? Mom raccoon will become pregnant between January and March. She will carry her young for about 63 days. She will find a safe place to make a den for her babies. The female raccoon can have between 3 and 6 babies.

Baby Raccoons

Did you know baby raccoons are called, kits or cubs? Baby raccoons are born very tiny - only 2 ounces in weight. They are blind and deaf. They are covered in light fur and their black masks are already showing. The kits are old enough to explore outside the den at 6 weeks of age.

Life of a Raccoon

Did you know most raccoons do not live past 3 years-old in the wild? Due to its many predators and even traffic in urban areas, the raccoon has a short lifespan. However, a healthy raccoon left alone can reach ages of 15 years in the wild. Some in captivity have lived even longer.

Quiz

Question 1: Where can the raccoon be found?

Answer 1: Throughout North America

Question 2: What facial feature does the raccoon have?

Answer 2: It has a black mask around its eyes

Question 3: What does the raccoon use its front paws for?

Answer 3: The sense of touch and to pick things up

Question 4: What other animal will the raccoon raid?

Answer 4: The raccoon likes to raid birds' nests

Question 5: What are baby raccoons called?

Answer 5: Kits or cubs

Thank you for checking out another addition from Sandie Lee Books! Make sure to check out Amazon.com for many other great titles.